*Axioms
of
Life*

Axioms of Life

Inspiring life principles gleaned from the magical moments of childhood...

Vijay Dandige

Copyright © 2016 by Vijay Dandige

All rights reserved. This book or any portion thereof may not be reproduced or used in any manner whatsoever without the express written permission of the publisher except for the use of brief quotations in a book review.

Printed in India

First Printing, 2016

ISBN-13: 978-1530728350

ISBN-10: 1530728355

Swami Publishing

355/A, M. A. K. Azad Road,

Gandhinagar, Nagpur, 440010 (India)

vijay.dandige@gmail.com

Acknowledgements

I would like to thank my buddies Arin and Riaan, who introduced me to my life's greatest joy, of being a grandfather and who also became the inspiration for my first book.

I would like to express my gratitude to Navin Athawale, a gentle soul and a fabulous designer, for designing the cover of this book.

I would also like to thank Neha Khanzode, Anju Koli Paturkar, Nachiketa Dandige and Kalpana Dandige for their help from time to time in the selection of quotes which make up the book's axioms.

And a big thanks, of course, to Nandini and Avinash Sahasrabudhe, who always show their enthusiastic appreciation and support in their own unique ways.

This book is fondly dedicated to my Facebook friends, especially to the ones listed below, whose 'Likes' and encouraging comments spurred me to go on and on and on.

Arin and Riaan

Smita Chaturvedi	Zofia Wegrzynowicz Bogiel	Meeta Menon Panday
Uttara Arkatkar	Megha Sharma Shende	Radhika Panday
Meera Joshi Diwadkar	Jaya Paturkar-Nighoskar	Pallavi Jain
Arijit Joshi	Jyoti Lahiri	Kalpana A. Koli
Richa Joshi	Arya Paturkar	Amit Mundada
Sandra Vsm	Nandini Sahasrabudhe	Anju Koli Paturkar
Deodatta Arkatkar	Neha Khanzode	Maithili Dandige
Mrunalini Tatke Vaidya	Shreeram Sahasrabudhe	Uttara Shrinivas
Ambica Desaraju	Nilesh Jaipurkar	Yogita Raut
Tulsi Keshkamat	Gita Rajagopalan	Archana Gupta
Praffull Kirpane	Kapil Gupta	Divya Shrotriya
Ketan Milind Panday	Aditya Paturkar	Kshama Bute
Neha Buwa Gogate	Sarang Dandige	Medha Dixit
Veena Puranik	Rashmi Panday	Anand Joshi
Devendra Rokde	Sanita Kumar	Bobbey Pawagi
Stephanie Ostrea	Madhavi Nighoskar	Ela Puri
Neeta Jog	Sanjeevani Tamaskar	Aniket Ramekar
Nilesh Manohar Gaidhane	Akshay A. Dudhakaware	Aleksandra Bogiel
Tanvi Arkatkar	Anil Ambadekar	Chinmay Dani
Amrita Prasad	Kasturi Sahasrabuddhe	Moira Kane
Mrudula Shahane	Nalini Ketan Panday	Pranjali Kadam
Ratan Panday	Anish Arkatkar	Arjun Vaidya
Balaji Ramasubramaniam	Jignesh Sanghvi	Prakash Badge
Prashant Upgade	Ritwik Panday	Shaunak Vaidya
Shrish Borkar	Anita Kurup	Anita Wilson
Aparna Sangitrao	Chhaya Naik	Abhilesh S. Wahane
Madhu Abrol	Mouli Gupta	Nandini Joshi
Rashmi Badge	Vishakha Pandharipande	Akbar H. Firdosy
Ameya Chaturvedi	Rkumar Iyer	Vijay Rathod
Isha Arkatkar	Meghna Mohril	Nupur Badge
Priya Padmanabhan	Ranjana Bobde	Shachi Arkatkar
Sonali Lanjewar Gaidhane	Varsha Deo	Sunanda Chaoji
Vijaya Shahane	Ajay Jain	Amitojas Dandige
Apoorva Mandloi	Ashwin Ingle	Gauri Shrotriya
Deepak Kaswa	Ian Kane	Kartikeya Chaturvedi
Kedar Ambokar	Malcolm Dias	Niranjan Markandeywar
Prabhat Tiwari	Pradeep Kale	Prakash Dixit
Rajan Patwardhan	Shreyas Sharma	Suresh Chikhlonde
Swanand Melag	Uday Shahane	Deepak Dhagamwar
Gazanfar Mirza	Raju Dahake	Swapna K. Gokhale
Geselle M Rodrigues	Meghana Panday	Vivek Deshpande
Chatudatta Arkatkar	Billy Cutler	Ashwin Sahasrabudhe
Avantika Ramekar	Shweta Waghmare	Nilesh Dandige

...and to
Mark Zuckerberg,
who's not a friend yet but who nonetheless made it all possible.

Preface

"Childhood is the most beautiful of all life's seasons."

-Anon

Indeed....childhood is the most magical, enchanting, exciting period of a person's life.... filled with love, happiness, joy.

It's a time for exploring, for creating, for discovering...for learning how to learn.

Childhood is when you are allowed to be a child: you are accepted for what you are...just the way you are. It's a time of blossoming, of being cared for, of being cherished.

Childhood is a world of magic and fantasy.

What makes childhood such a wonderfully special part of life?

It's because children come naturally endowed with certain qualities - pristine qualities really - that help them see their surrounding world and react to it in amazing ways.

Children possess, among others, an innate simplicity: naturalness, which gives them pure, innocent, open and natural hearts. And this, in turn, makes them flexible and ever ready to learn and to grow.

They always live, fully, in the present moment and don't take life seriously.

They are equipped with an inherent sense of wonder; everything amazes them; they look at the world with new eyes.

They are endlessly curious and fire a barrage of questions. This inordinate curiosity opens up the world for them, it galvanises their creativity and spurs their imagination.

Kids have persistence, and do not quit easily: they are relentless until their demands are met.

Children lead excitement-filled lives. They can get excited about the smallest of things. For them any activity turns into a new adventure, a chance to explore, a new fun, an interesting challenge.

They are naturally happy. Their happiness is not dependent upon others; they create their own happiness out of their own choice. And they have an unlimited capacity to love. Most children readily accept and give open, spontaneous, unconditional love.

They also possess a vibrant sense of their own worth and potential: they instinctively know they are important. They have an innate sense of wisdom, too - wisdom that is based on what they have learnt from their own experiences. For them most things are pretty straightforward: right or wrong. And they have a sense of the fundamental unity of life. Like most adults, they are not dogged by feelings of separateness: you-and-me or they-and-me.

Children are blessed with short memories which equip them with the ability to live from one experience to another, to let things go and just live. This quality also makes them forgiving. Because they don't hold grudges, forgiving comes easily to them.

Another outstanding quality is their natural, deep and abiding trust. They trust their parents fully.

Best of all, children excel in play and imagination. First, they use playing as a means to make friends and bond. Playing together with other children breeds healthy interactions and relationships.

Second, play and imagination boosts their creativity. Children are endlessly creative. They have a natural tendency to daydream and wonder, and they use their imaginations freely. Their limitless imagination is not constrained by inhibitions or rules or thoughts of being wrong or what others might think or expectations or results. This makes their creativity wild and fantastic, a pure joy and fun. Their habit of 'pretending': imaginative play - being a superhero or a princess - helps them come up with alternative ways of being, and seeing an issue, in more creative ways.

That children are incredibly creative has been acknowledged by leading scientists, artists and experts.

Albert Einstein said, "To stimulate creativity, one must develop the childlike inclination for play and the childlike desire for recognition."

Pablo Picasso said, "Every child is an artist. The problem is how to remain an artist once we grow up."

And Robert Oppenheimer, father of the atomic bomb, said, "There are children playing in the street who could solve some of my top problems in physics, because they have modes of sensory perception that I lost long ago."

Childhood...indeed... is the best of all life's seasons.

As dramatist Eugene Ionesco said, "Childhood is the world of miracle and wonder; as if creation rose, bathed in the light, out of the darkness, utterly new and fresh and astonishing...."

But alas......!

This magical season is short-lived.

And that is one of the greatest tragedies of life.

In the inexorable tumult of growing up, these pristine qualities of childhood get replaced by a host of negative, life-draining traits, and qualities: worry, anxiety, jealousy, competitiveness, selfishness, greed, doubts and distrust, fears, inhibitions, lack of self-esteem, phoniness... et al.

Leaving their magical qualities behind.... the child of yesterday becomes the adult of today.

----- o -----

This book came about by a happy chance. Last year I was looking at some photos of my 15-months-old grandson. In one picture, he had climbed into a big carton and was sitting there with a huge smile on his face.

And the thought came to me: "How readily children do whatever makes them happy" - something that we adults fail, so many times, to do.

And that became an axiom of life.

Then I looked carefully at other photos of my grandson and his big brother, to see whether any of them hinted at or suggested truths or axioms relating to life. I found plenty.

The two children in the book are my grandsons, the younger one, Riaan and his older brother, Arin Sahasrabudhe.

Although this might appear a children's book, it is actually meant for us adult.

There is a weird irony about life.

Children, even while having their magical qualities, daydream of someday becoming adults.

While the adults themselves, caught in the throes of their worldly struggles, conflicts and complexities, look longingly back to the days of their own childhood and pine for the simplicity, naturalness and happiness they once possessed - and lost.

If we could rediscover some of the pure, enchanting qualities of our childhood - even in small measure - from under the deluge of negative attributes and emotions we have accumulated as adults over the years.... we could redeem and enrich our lives.

And that is the humble aspiration of this book - to inspire us to find and embrace the child within each one of us.

Vijay Dandige

Nagpur, India

Axioms of Life

Axiom # 1 of Life

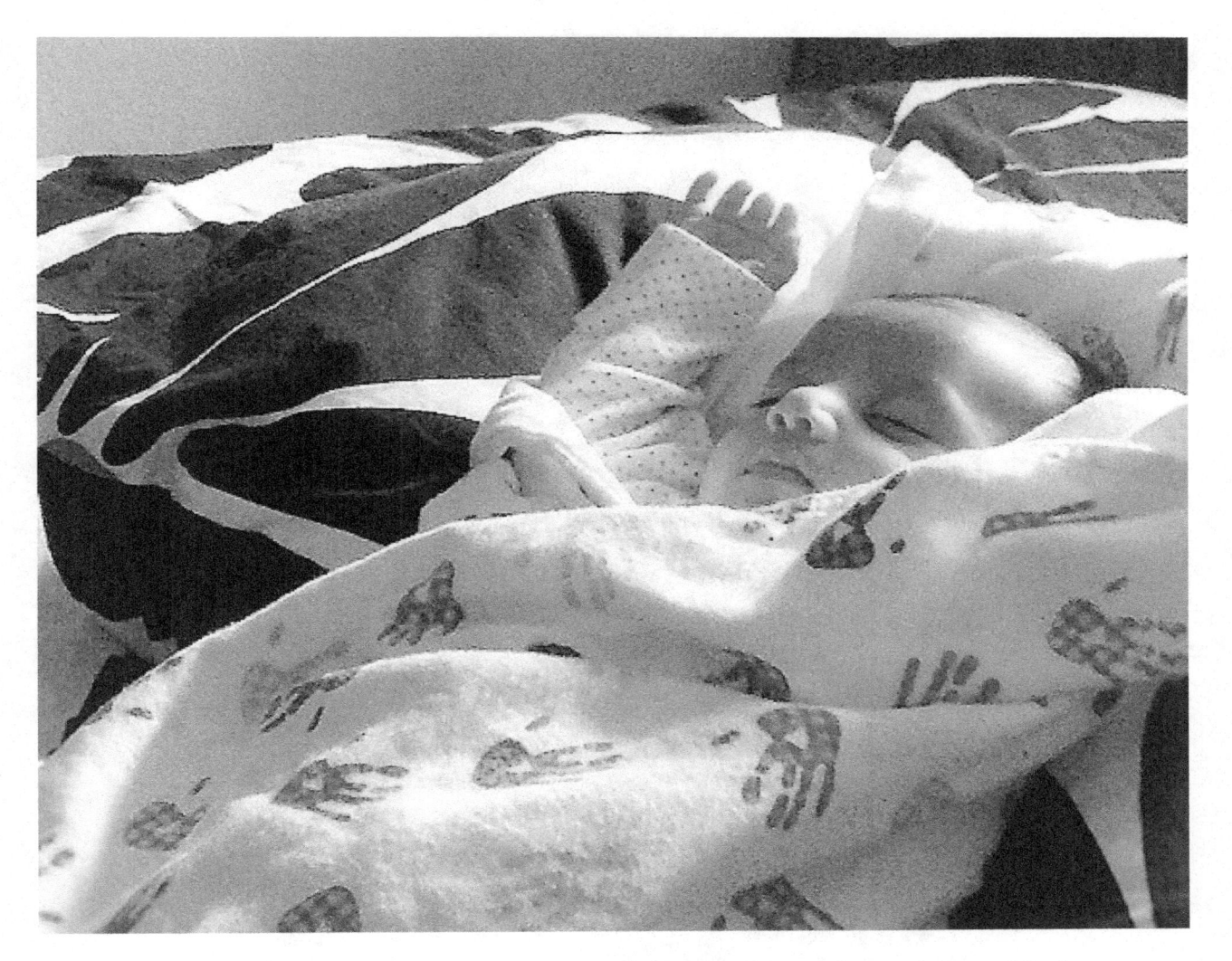

Life begins with a blessing itself: the gift of life from parents.

Axiom # 2 of Life

The second greatest gift from parents: a big brother to watch over you.

Axiom # 3 of Life

"There is no way to happiness. Happiness is the way."

- Buddha

Axiom # 4 of Life

Remember, "the usefulness of a cup is in its emptiness": empty yourself of all preconceived conclusions and open yourself to everything and everyone.

-Bruce Lee

Axiom # 5 of Life

"The difference between something good and something great is attention to detail."

- Charles R. Swindoll

Axiom # 6 of Life

"Look at life through the windshield, not the rear-view mirror."

- Byrd Baggett

Axiom # 7 of Life

"A good life is when you smile often, dream big, laugh a lot and realise how blessed you are for what you have."

- Anon

Axiom # 8 of Life

"Never put off till tomorrow the fun you can have today."

- Aldous Huxley

Axiom # 9 of Life

When life's problems become too knotty and vexing...
solutions can be found with deep thinking.

Axiom # 10 of Life

"Life is like a balloon. If you never let yourself go, you'll never know how far you can rise."

- Linda Poindexter

Axiom # 11 of Life

When you turn the page of a book, you start on a thrilling journey of a lifetime – a journey like no other.

Axiom # 12 of Life

Have at least one true friend in life who will always have your back, no matter how badly things may go.

Axiom # 13 of Life

"Life is just a mirror, and what you see out there, you must first see inside of you."

- Wally Amos

Axiom # 14 of Life

Always be self-reliant. Do your duties cheerfully.

Axiom # 15 of Life

Rekindle your sense of wonder.

Axiom # 16 of Life

Even if people call you a nerd or a geek, remember it pays to be a techie in today's world.

Axiom # 17 of Life

Always drink your fill of love, joy, happiness, fun, friendship, milk, honey and all the other blessings of life.

Axiom # 18 of Life

Give full expression to your own unique nature.

Axiom # 19 of Life

Be good at housekeeping: a place for everything and everything in its place.

Axiom # 20 of Life

Seek and you will find.

Axiom # 21 of Life

[Like the squirrel that unwittingly] "plants trees - she buries nuts, then forgets where she hid them - do good and forget."

- Anon

Axiom # 22 of Life

"It's more than okay sometimes to get angry. It's part of being really alive."

- Deborah Fox

Axiom # 23 of Life

Remember, "a book is a gift you can open again and again."

- Garrison Keillor

Axiom # 24 of Life

Always carry your childhood with you, for "childhood is the most beautiful of all life's seasons."

- Anon

Axiom # 25 of Life

[Cherish your] "special moments: each one counts; hold on to them for memories that will last you for eternities."

- Anon

Axiom # 26 of Life

[Always] "love the people [you] can be crazy with."

- Anon

Axiom # 27 of Life

If you have to display anything at all, display your books because they "prove you are a reader - someone who lives a thousand lives before he dies."

- George R. R. Martin

Axiom # 28 of Life

Remember, the bars that you think keep you captive exist only in your mind. You can always find a way to break free.

Axiom # 29 of Life

When you wear it, "cock your hat - angles are attitudes."
- Frank Sinatra

Axiom # 30 of Life

Don't look over the fence to see if the grass is greener on the other side. Just keep on watering yours.

Axiom # 31 of Life

[Never] "cry over [whatever is spilt.] "Clean it up and move on. You still have living to do."

- Anon

Axiom # 32 of Life

Remember, "if you're wasting time having fun, you're not wasting time."

- Tim Ferriss

Axiom # 33 of Life

Even as you soak in the sunrays from outside, never forget that "within you is the light of a thousand suns."

- Robert Adams

Axiom # 34 of Life

Every so often, it's a good idea to sit quietly amidst trees, listening to the soothing sounds of nature rather than the shrill, chaotic din of city traffic.

Axiom # 35 of Life

[Find] "a soul you can connect with on every level."

- Anon

Axiom # 36 of Life

Remember, "you don't have to brush all your teeth - just the ones you want to keep."

- Anon

Axiom # 37 of Life

Do whatever makes you happy.

Axiom # 38 of Life

Do your own thing. Don't copy others.

Axiom # 39 of Life

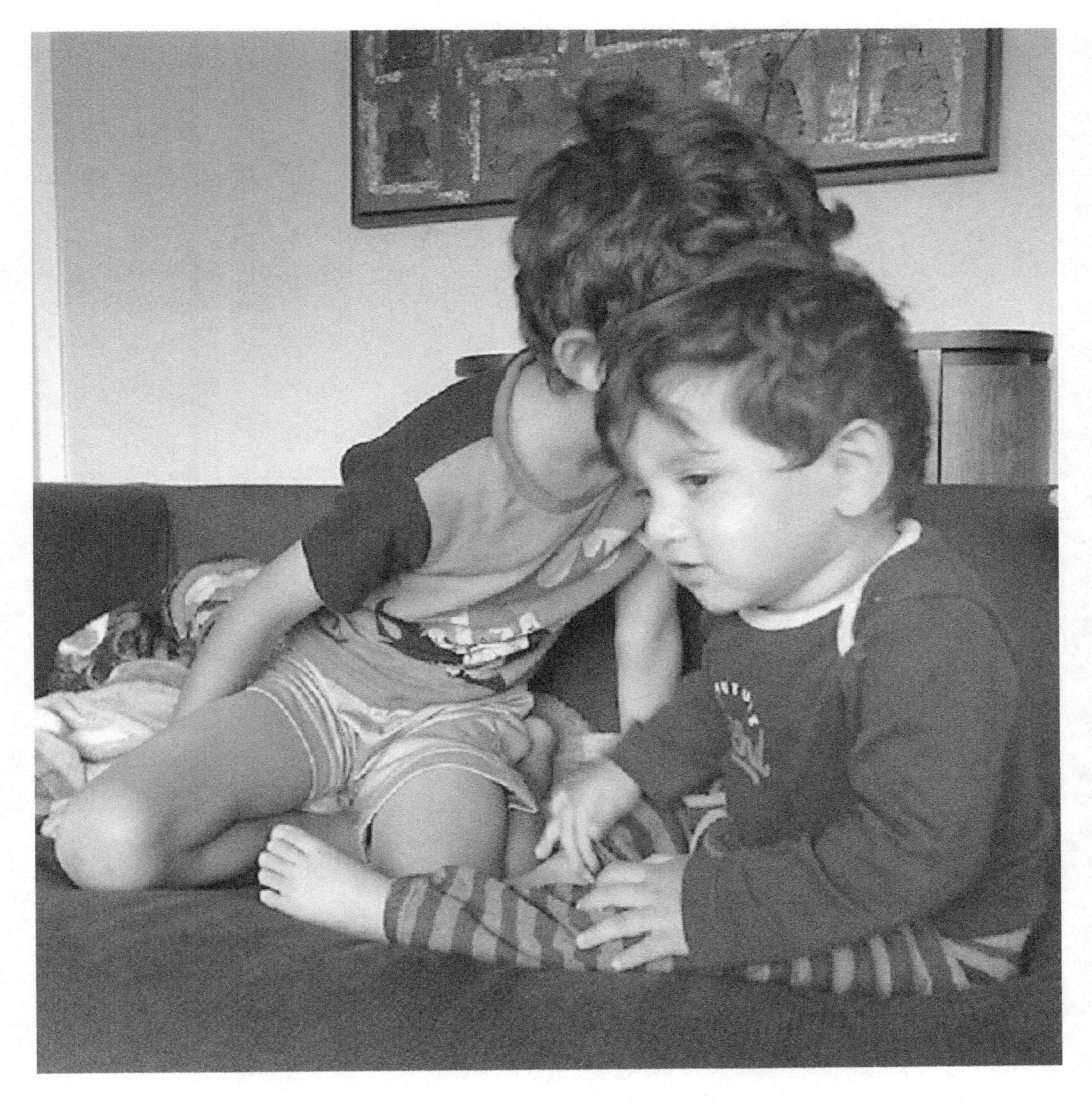

"A true relationship is when you can tell each other anything and everything. No secrets. No lies."

-Anon

Axiom # 40 of Life

"Sometimes, you need to look at life from a different perspective."

- Inas Chahboun

Axiom # 41 of Life

Never reach the stage where you are "bored of being bored...because being bored is boring."

- Anon

Axiom # 42 of Life

"Kindness is like coffee. It awakens your spirit and improves your day. Fill your cup with both."

- Anon

Axiom # 43 of Life

Never forget: "[you] do not stop playing because [you] grow old, [you] grow old because [you] stop playing."

- George Bernard Shaw

Axiom # 44 of Life

Climbing for your goal only affirms that you are trying harder...and not giving up.

Axiom # 45 of Life

Remember, "just as hard as you work out at the gym, it's just as hard working in the kitchen."

- Anon

Axiom # 46 of Life

Technology is fine ...and even as "your fingers get more skilled on a keypad, [remember never] to lose the art of holding the pen."

- Anon

Axiom # 47 of Life

"You can have a whole new outlook on life when you look at it from another angle."

- Nigel McKain

Axiom # 48 of Life

You learn best when you learn together.

Axiom # 49 of Life

"Push yourself because no one else is going to do it for you."

- Anon

Axiom # 50 of Life

"Listen to your inner genius. Those who do, often end up changing the world."

- Duane Marino

Axiom # 51 of Life

"Accept your burden and carry it with joy."

- John Ajvide Lindqvist

Axiom # 52 of Life

Remember, the difference between being well dressed and wearing a costume. "Clothes make a statement, costumes tell a story."

- Mason Cooley

Axiom # 53 of Life

Falling down is not failure. Failure is not getting up again.

Axiom # 54 of Life

Remember, "you can't have two faces under one hat."

- Jamaican proverb

Axiom # 55 of Life

Remember, "junk food satisfies you for a minute. Being fit satisfies you for life."

- Anon

Axiom # 56 of Life

"Be bold. Be strong. Be brave. Be happy. Be free. Be silly. Be original. Be you."

- Anon

Axiom # 57 of Life

"Life is a party. Dress like it."

- Lilly Pulitzer

Axiom # 58 of Life

If you want to revitalise your soul, work in the garden - "for gardening is a metaphor for life, teaching you to nourish new life and weed out that which doesn't succeed."

- Nelson Mandela

Axiom # 59 of Life

"Life is like riding a bicycle. To keep your balance, you must keep moving."

- Albert Einstein

Axiom # 60 of Life

True friendship is being together, doing nothing and still enjoying every moment of it.

Axiom # 61 of Life

"Life is like a game of tennis: the player who serves well seldom loses."

-Anon

Axiom # 62 of Life

"The healthiest relationships are those where you are a team; where you protect each other and stand up for one another."

- Sharon Rivkin

Axiom # 63 of Life

Remember, "like a piece in a puzzle, you have a unique position to occupy."

- Anon

Axiom # 64 of Life

"There is no other love like the love of a big brother."

- Astrid Alauda

Axiom # 65 of Life

"Don't start your day with the broken pieces of yesterday. Every day is a fresh start, a new beginning. Every morning you wake up is the first day of your new life."

- Anon

Axiom # 66 of Life

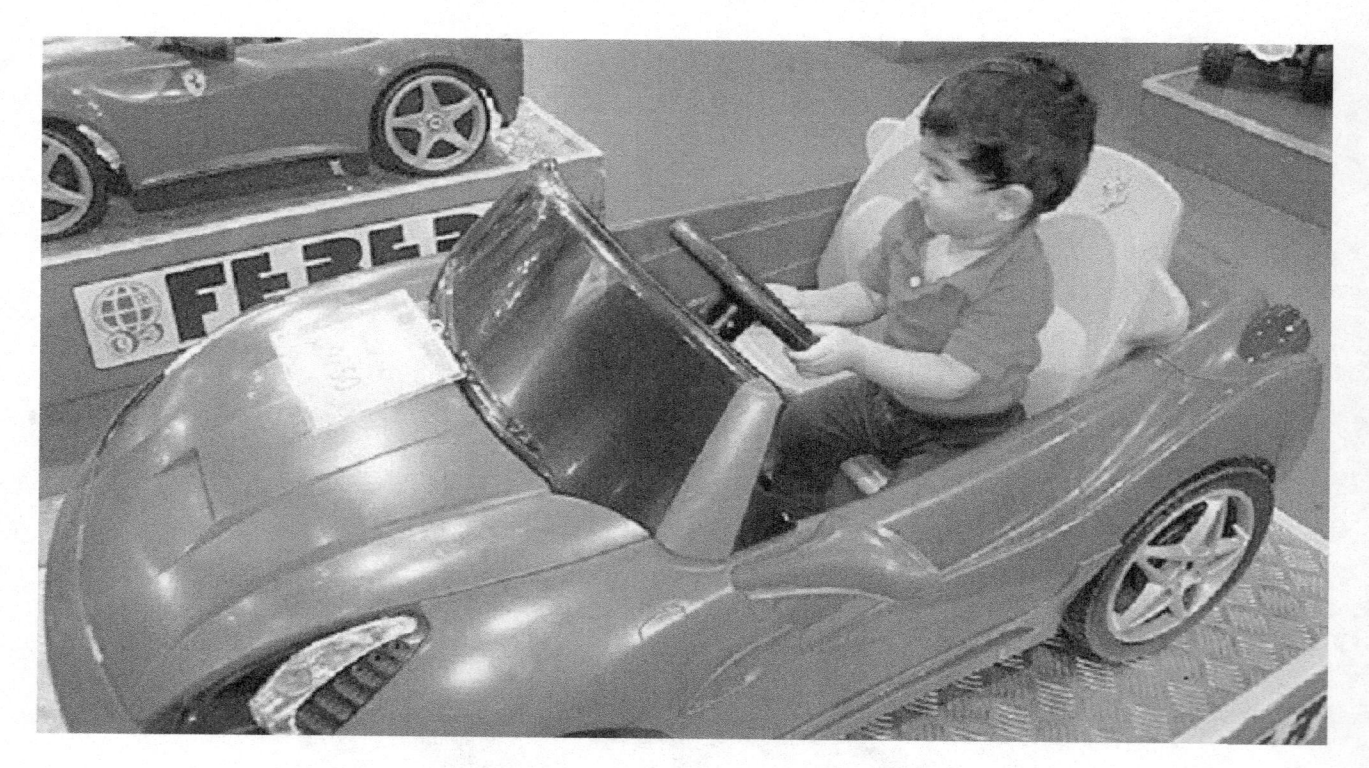

Always choose your car carefully: it's an extension of your personality, it symbolises personal freedom.

Axiom # 67 of Life

"One of the best feelings in the world is when you hug someone you love, and they hug you back even tighter."

- Anon

Axiom # 68 of Life

"Don't let anyone tell you that daydreaming is a waste of time." Remember, "everything starts as somebody's daydream."

- Susan Miller and Larry Niven

Axiom # 69 of Life

"Sometimes, the smallest things take up the most room in your heart."

- A. A. Milne, Winnie the Pooh

Axiom # 70 of Life

"People will forget what you said, people will forget what you did, but people will never forget how you made them feel."

- Maya Angelou

Axiom # 71 of Life

"If all you can do is crawl, start crawling."

- Rumi

Axiom # 72 of Life

"Whatever good things [you] build end up building [you]."

- Jim Rohn

Axiom # 73 of Life

"Fitness is not about being better than someone else. It's about being better than you used to be."

- Brett Hoebel

Axiom # 74 of Life

"If you don't do crazy things while you're young, you'll have nothing to smile about when you're old."

- Anon

Axiom # 75 of Life

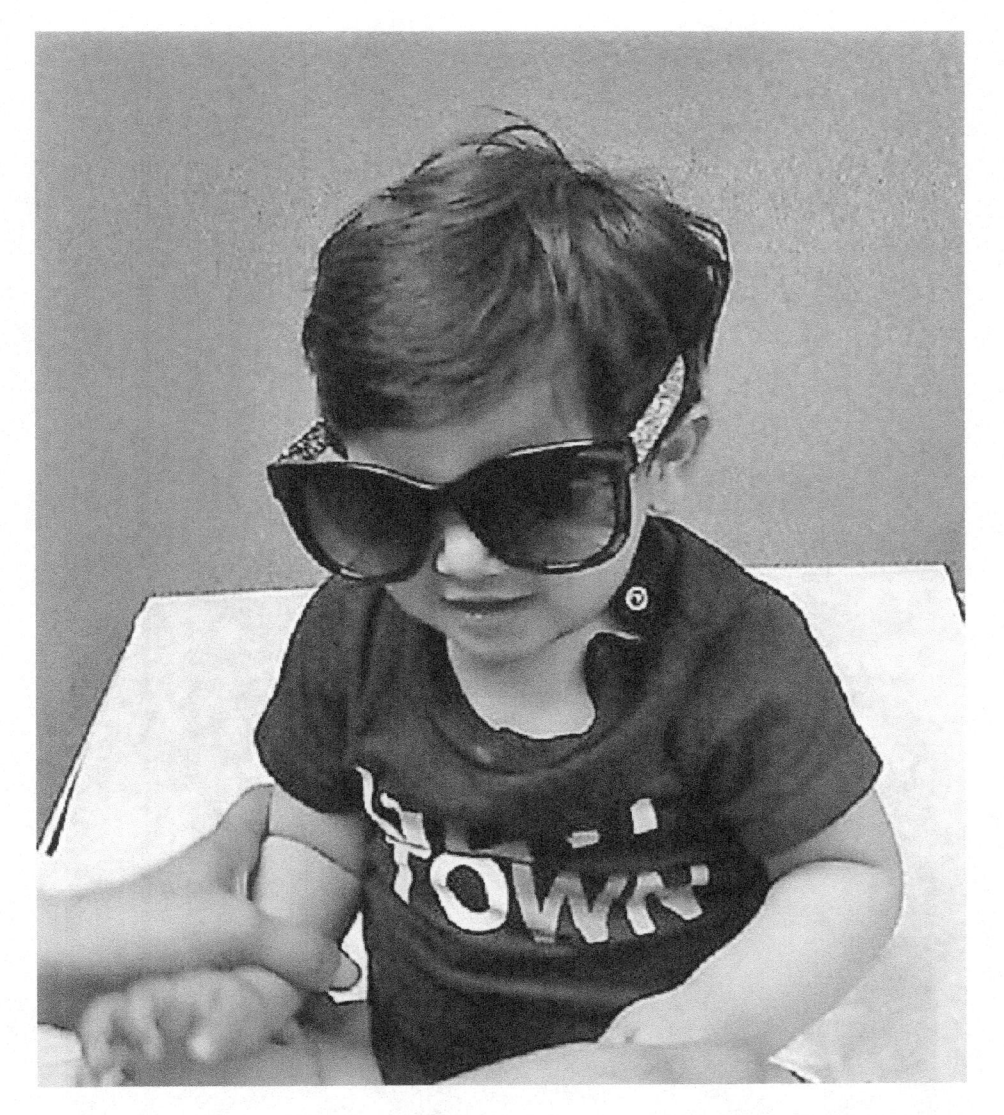

"Don't change to fit the fashion. Change the fashion to fit you."

- Anon

Axiom # 76 of Life

Always begin your journey with a small step.

Axiom # 77 of Life

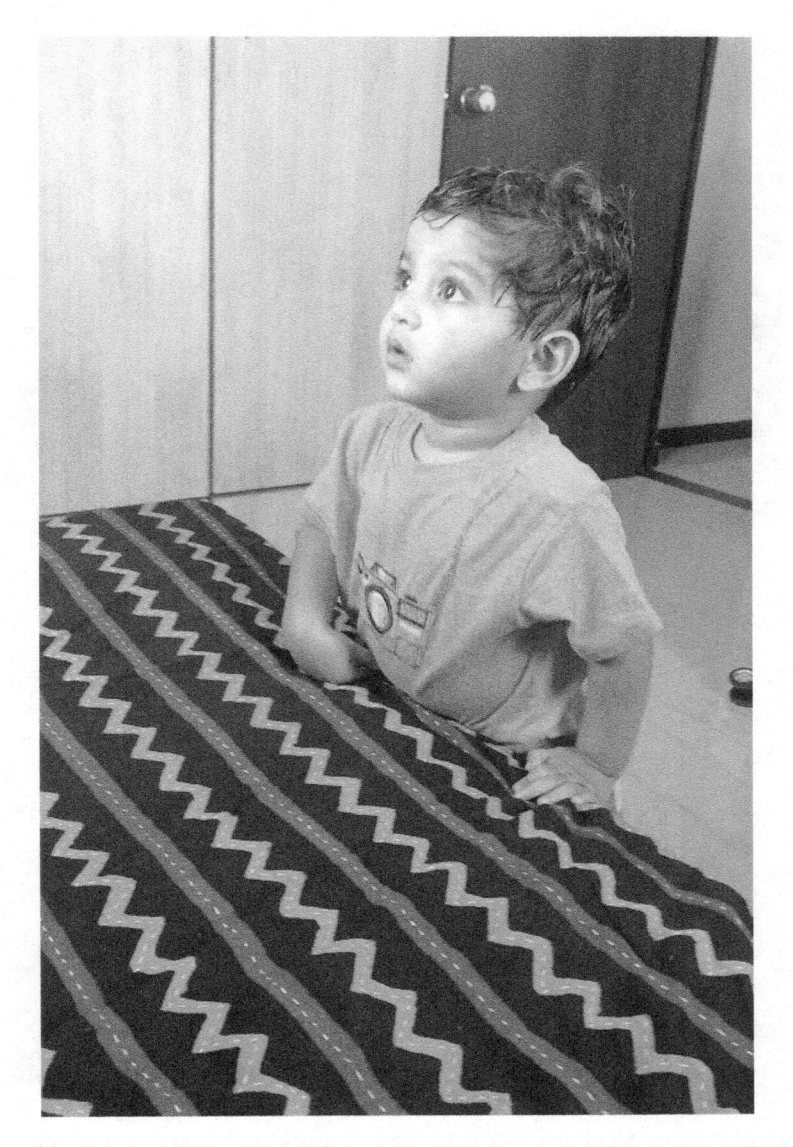

Remember, "the key to success in life is to have a clear vision of your goal, and not look in any direction but ahead."

- Lauren Nesselroad

Axiom # 78 of Life

"Style is knowing who you are, what you want to say and not giving a damn."

- Orson Wells

Axiom # 79 of Life

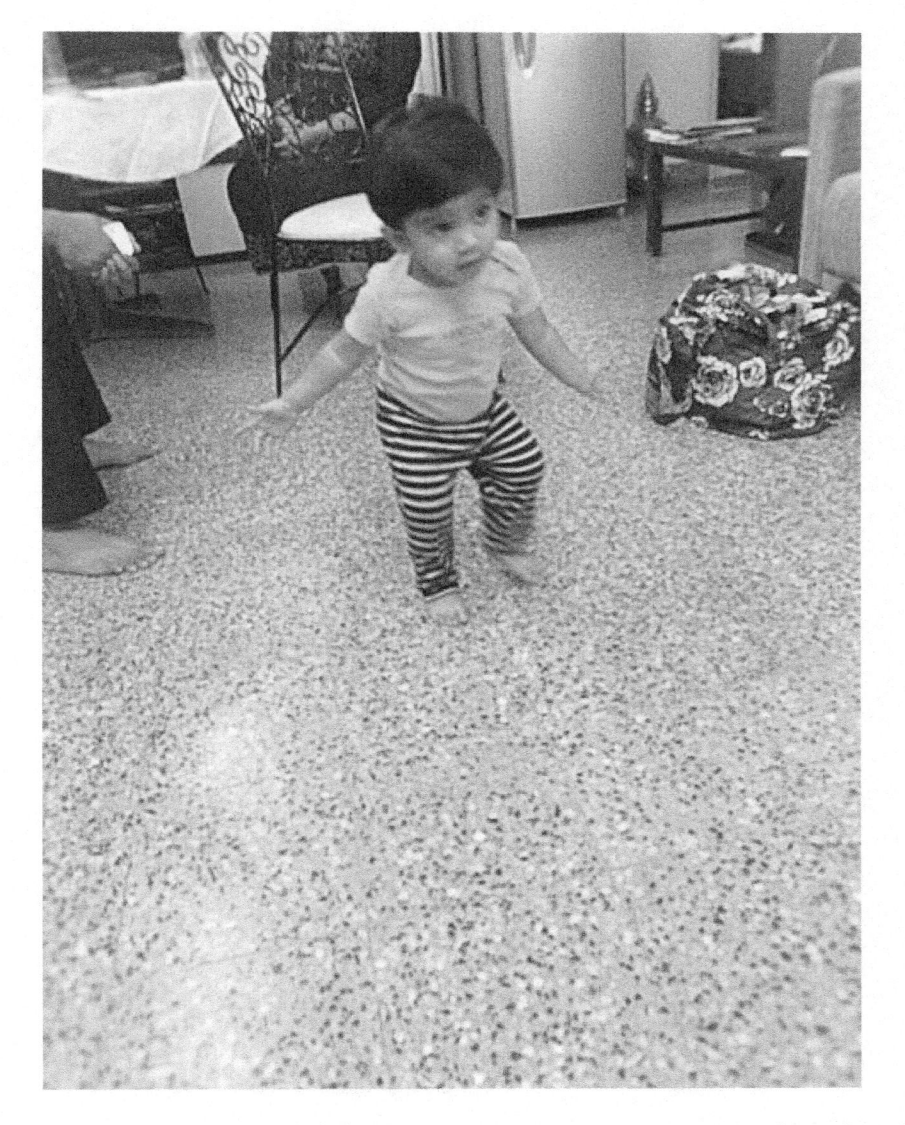

Dance for yourself - always. "Dance is the hidden language of the soul" and a shortcut to happiness.

- Martha Graham

Axiom # 80 of Life

Always "look up to the sky. You'll never find a rainbow if you're looking down."

- Charles Chaplin

Axiom # 81 of Life

Remember, "when you try to control everything, you enjoy nothing. Sometimes, you just need to relax, breathe, let go and just live in the moment."

- Anon

Axiom # 82 of Life

If you have found your true love, cherish them with your heart and soul. True love is a rare jewel.

Axiom # 83 of Life

Remember, "a good [travelling] companion shortens the longest road."

- Turkish proverb

Axiom # 84 of Life

"What you hope ever to do with ease, you must learn first to do with diligence."

- Samuel Johnson

Axiom # 85 of Life

Like the fish in the tank..."it's better to be a big fish in a small pond than a small fish in a mighty ocean."

- Proverb

Axiom # 86 of Life

"Happiness is sand between [your] toes and a sunburn on [your] nose."

- Anon

Axiom # 87 of Life

[As you grow up], "you realise it becomes less important to have more friends, and more important to have real ones."

-Anon

Axiom # 88 of Life

Remember, "life is like a steering wheel: it only takes one small move to change your entire direction."

- Kellie Elmore

Axiom # 89 of Life

Keep "[your] house clean enough to be healthy and dirty enough to be happy."

- Anon

Axiom # 90 of Life

"Wearing a hat versus not wearing a hat is the difference between looking adequate and looking your best."

- Martha Sliter

Axiom # 91 of Life

"Best friends are the ones who are there: whenever, wherever, however, and most importantly, forever."

- Anon

Axiom # 92 of Life

"Life is like a hot bath. It feels good while you are in it, but the longer you stay in, the more wrinkled you get."

- Anon

Axiom # 93 of Life

"A day in the sand is a beautiful day."

- Anon

Axiom # 94 of Life

Always work to save your planet. "When it's time to take out the trash, remember to 'reduce, reuse, recycle.'"

- Anon

Axiom # 95 of Life

"Not until we are lost [in thoughts] do we begin to understand [life.]"

- Henry David Thoreau

Axiom # 96 of Life

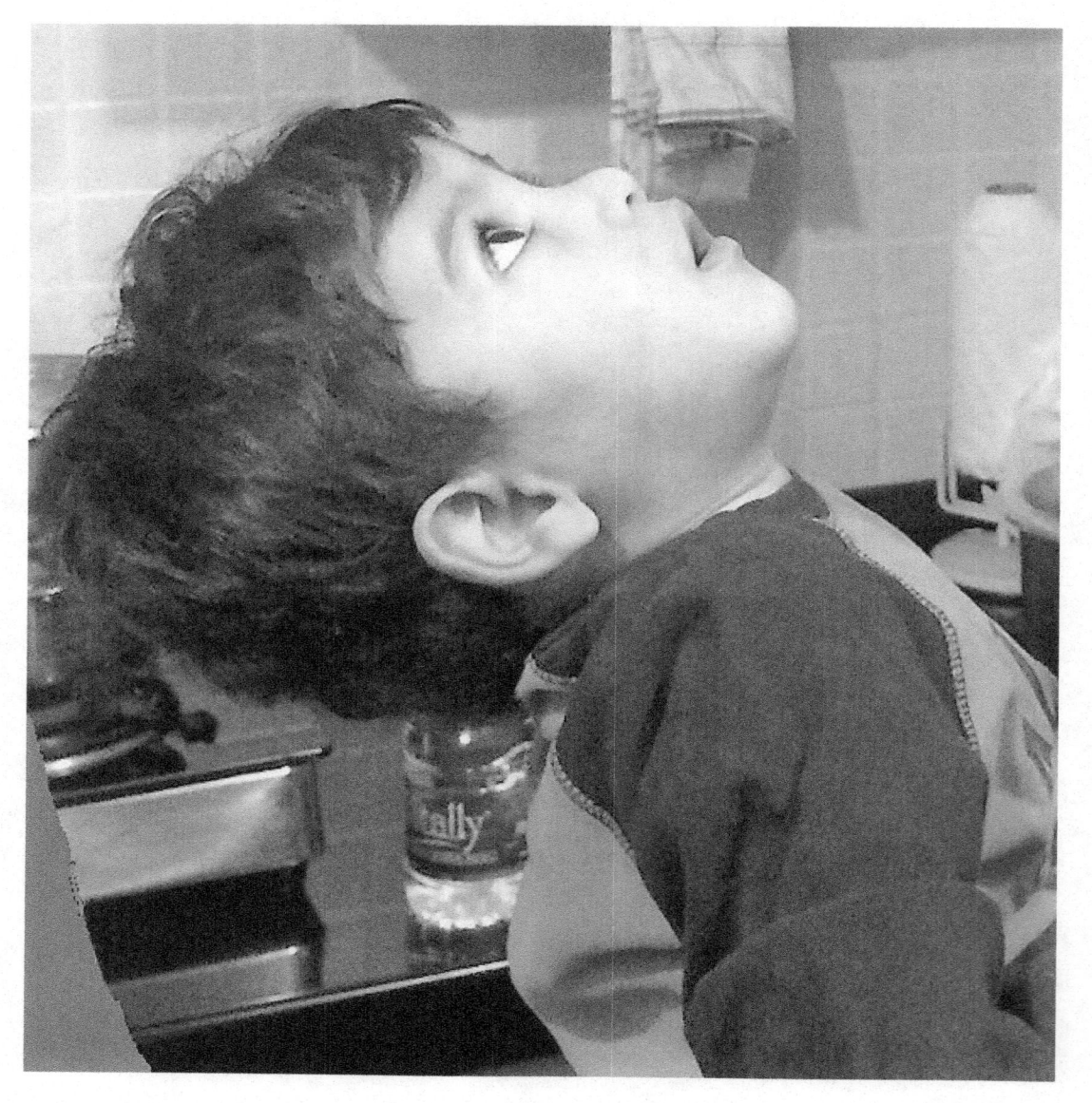

Remember, "it's hard to be down when you are looking up."

- Anon

Axiom # 97 of Life

"If you want to [ride the waves], you must be willing to step out of the boat."

- John Ortberg

Axiom # 98 of Life

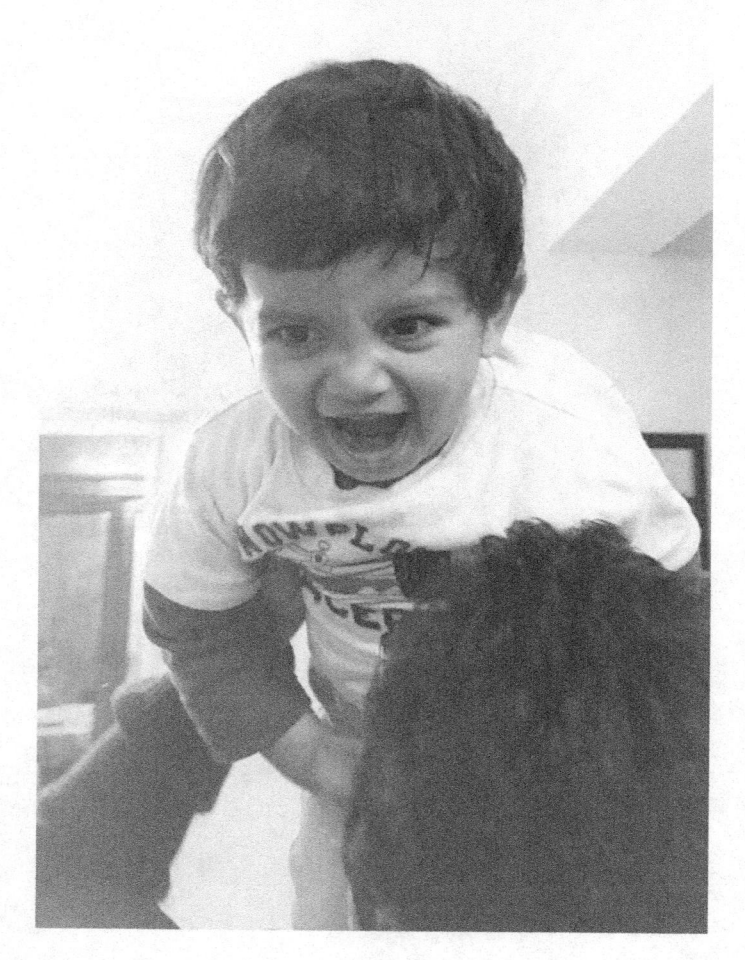

Every so often, have "a hearty laugh and laugh with all your heart. A good hearty laugh does wonders for your body and soul."

- Anon

Axiom # 103 of Life

Whenever you eat anything, apply this rule: "if it came from a plant, eat it; if it was made in a plant, don't."

- Michael Pollan

Axiom # 104 of Life

Remember, "being well dressed is a beautiful form of politeness."

- Anon

Axiom # 105 of Life

"Life is like driving a car. It's okay to look behind sometimes, but keep looking straight because life goes on."

- Cynthia Tjoe

Axiom # 106 of Life

Never forget ..."technology is a useful servant but a dangerous master".... best used just for everyday learning.

- Christian Lous Lange

Axiom # 107 of Life

Remember, "the food you eat can either be the safest and most powerful form of medicine or the slowest form of poison."

- Ann Wigmore

Axiom # 108 of Life

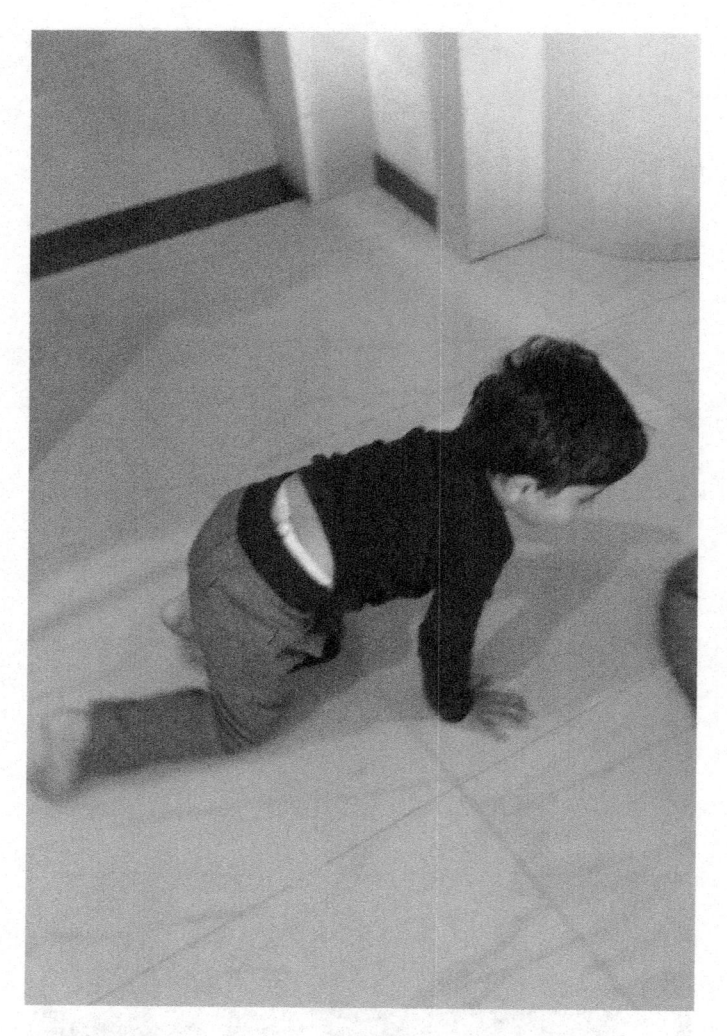

"If you can't fly, then run, if you can't run, then walk, if you can't walk, then crawl, but whatever you do, you have to keep moving forward."

- Martin Luther King Jr.

Axiom # 109 of Life

Make sure you have someone to lend you a helping hand when you tumble down.

Axiom # 110 of Life

"Play in the dirt because life is too short to always have clean fingernails."

- Anon

Axiom # 111 of Life

Remember, "the telephone is a good way to talk to people without having to offer them a drink."

-Fran Lobowitz

Axiom # 112 of Life

Ecstasy is relaxing on a sofa, stretching your legs and devouring your favourite snack.

Axiom # 113 of Life

"When everything seems to be going against you, remember that the plane takes off against the wind, not with it."

- Henry Ford

Axiom # 114 of Life

Be like the lamp that welcomes you at the doorstep: "burn [yourself] up to give light to others."

- Anon

Axiom # 115 of Life

"When you [are ready to] dance to your own rhythm, life [begins to] tap its toes to your beat."

- Terri Guillemets

Axiom # 116 of Life

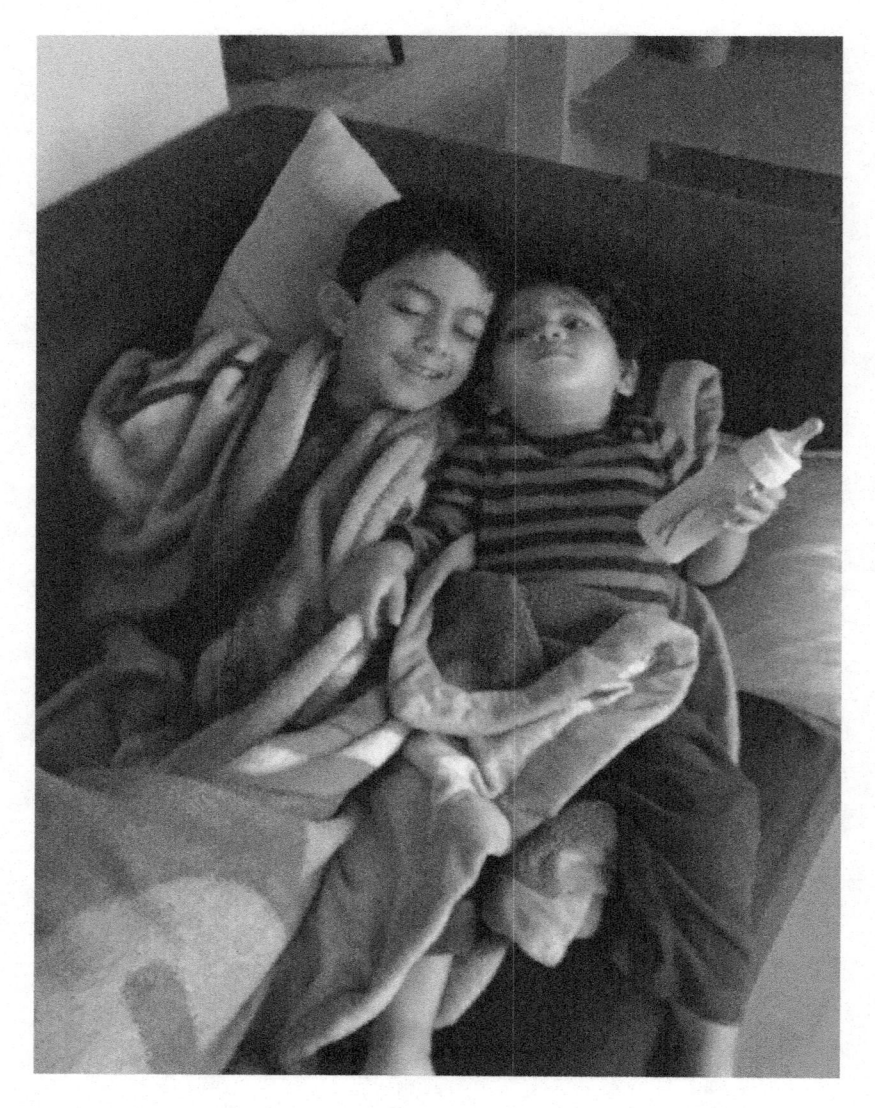

Remember, "a good friend knows all your stories. A best friend has lived them with you."

-Anon

Axiom # 117 of Life

"It doesn't matter where you are going. It's who you have beside you."

- Anon

Axiom # 118 of Life

"Always remember to fall asleep with a dream and wake up with a purpose."

- Anon

Axiom # 119 of Life

"[You] may have friends all over the world. But very few will truly know your heart."

- Chinese proverb

Axiom # 120 of Life

Be like a hen. Remember "the rooster may crow, but the hen delivers the goods."

- Anon

Axiom # 121 of Life

"You can find magic wherever you look. Sit back and relax, all you need is a book."

- Dr. Seuss

Axiom # 122 of Life

Remember, "attitude is a little thing that makes a big difference."

- Winston Churchill

Axiom # 123 of Life

"Nothing - not a conversation, not a handshake or even a hug - establishes friendship so forcefully as eating together."

- Jonathan Safran Foer

Axiom # 124 of Life

"Being organised isn't just about moving stuff around. It's about changing the way you think and building new habits."

- Anon

Axiom # 125 of Life

Happiness is a spoonful of ice cream dripping down your mouth.

Axiom # 126 of Life

"Friendship isn't about whom you have known the longest. It's about who came, and never left your side."

- Anon

Axiom # 127 of Life

"Don't watch the clock. Do what it does. Keep going."

- Sam Levenson

Axiom # 128 of Life

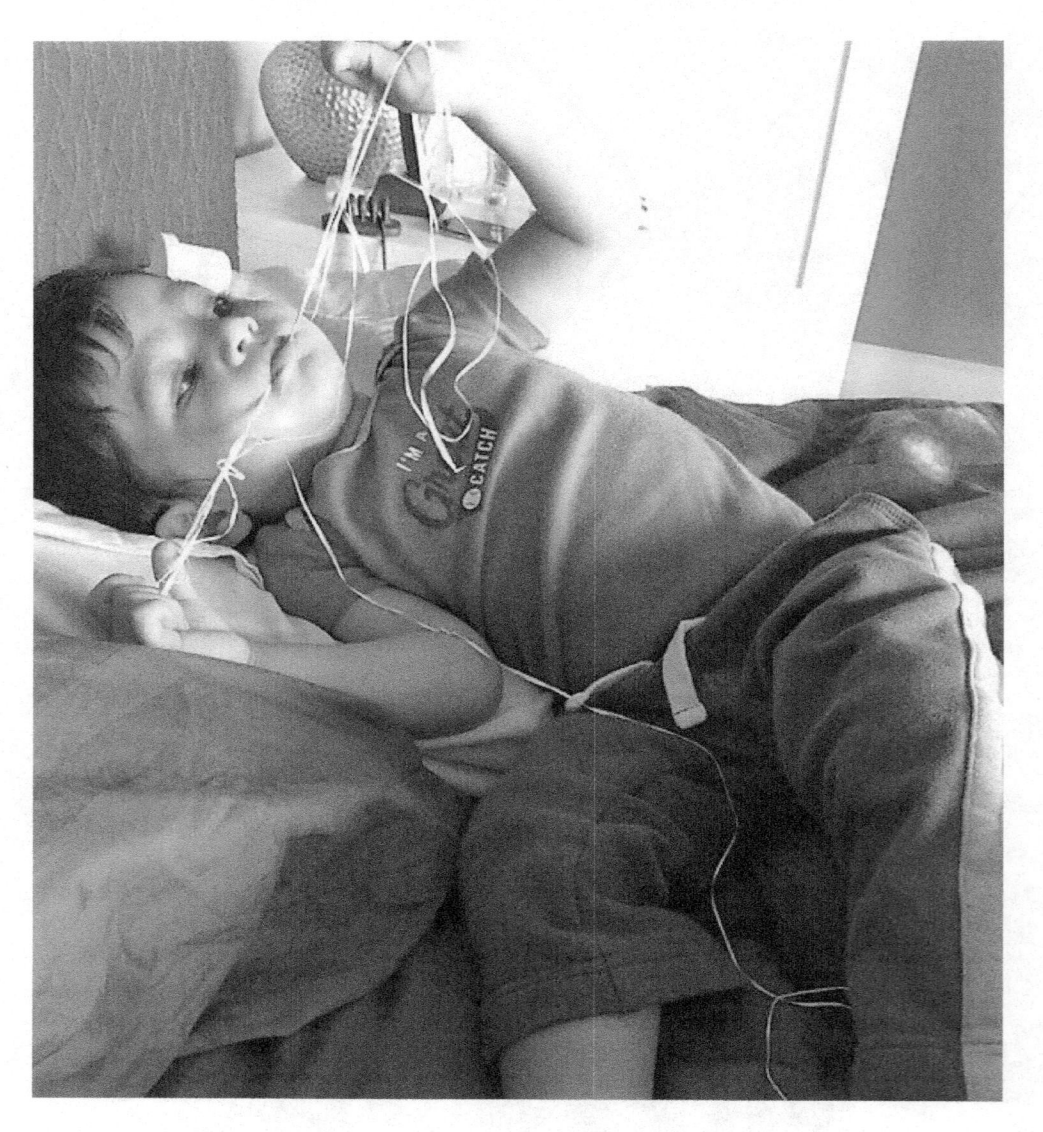

Remember, "each one of us is a unique thread, woven into the beautiful fabric of, our collective consciousness."

- Jaeda DeWalt

Axiom # 129 of Life

[Even as you stand before it], "recognise that fish as a member of [your] invisible family - not as your equal ...... but as another being that [is your] concern."

-Jonathan Safran Foer

Axiom # 130 of Life

"Happiness is doing something stupid and laughing about it for weeks."

- Anon

Axiom # 131 of Life

Remember, "stories make you think and dream; books make you want to ask questions."

-Michael Morpurgo

Axiom # 132 of Life

"The future lies before you, like a field of fallen snow; be careful how you tread it, for every step will show."

- Anon

References

A. A. Milne, W. t. (n.d.). Retrieved from www.etsy.com
Adams, R. (n.d.). Retrieved from inspiringheights.co.in
Alauda, A. (n.d.). Retrieved from quotesgram.com
Amos, W. (n.d.). Retrieved from www.flickr.com
Angelou, M. (n.d.). Retrieved from quotefancy.com
Anon. (n.d.). Retrieved from www.quoteswarehouse.com
Anon. (n.d.). Retrieved from www.pinterest.com
Anon. (n.d.). Retrieved from www.picturequotes.com
Anon. (n.d.). Retrieved from quotepix.com
Anon. (n.d.). Retrieved from www.pinterest.com
Anon. (n.d.). Retrieved from breakupquotes.com
Anon. (n.d.). Retrieved from feelmylove.org
Anon. (n.d.). Retrieved from quotesgram.com
Anon. (n.d.). Retrieved from rowdymclean.com
Anon. (n.d.). Retrieved from whisper.sh
Anon. (n.d.). Retrieved from wanelo.com
Anon. (n.d.). Retrieved from www.etsy.com
Anon. (n.d.). Retrieved from www.pinterest.com
Anon. (n.d.). Retrieved from www.dailyhappyquotes.com
Anon. (n.d.). Retrieved from www.firstcovers.com
Anon. (n.d.). Retrieved from gardentherapy.ca
Anon. (n.d.). Retrieved from www.tenniscanada.com
Anon. (n.d.). Retrieved from howtobehappy.guru
Anon. (n.d.). Retrieved from free-quotes.xyz
Anon. (n.d.). Retrieved from rawforbeauty.com
Anon. (n.d.). Retrieved from www.pixteller.com
Anon. (n.d.). Retrieved from www.lifetasteswell.com
Anon. (n.d.). Retrieved from www.quoteistan.com
Anon. (n.d.). Retrieved from www.thequotepedia.com
Anon. (n.d.). Retrieved from weheartit.com
Anon. (n.d.). Retrieved from www.pinterest.com
Anon. (n.d.). Retrieved from www.pinterest.com
Anon. (n.d.). Retrieved from www.benfrancia.com
Anon. (n.d.). Retrieved from www.pinterest.com
Anon. (n.d.). Retrieved from www.benfrancia.com
Anon. (n.d.). Retrieved from www.pinterest.com
Anon. (n.d.). Retrieved from https://www.instagram.com/p/_8dQi8kTZr/
Anon. (n.d.). Retrieved from quotesgram.com

Anon. (n.d.). Retrieved from www.pinterest.com
Anon. (n.d.). Retrieved from pinterest.com
Anon. (n.d.). Retrieved from lilluna.com
Anon. (n.d.). Retrieved from www.stylehasnosize.com
Anon. (n.d.). Retrieved from www.pinterest.com
Anon. (n.d.). Retrieved from http://www.fitnessquotesimg.com
Anon. (n.d.). Retrieved from quotesgram.com
Anon. (n.d.). Retrieved from www.thequotepedia.com
Anon. (n.d.). Retrieved from Kushandwizdom, www.pinterest.com
Anon. (n.d.). Retrieved from Kushandwizdom, www.pinterest.com
Baggett, B. (n.d.). Retrieved from www.quotesvalley.com
Buddha. (n.d.). Retrieved from www.quotesvalley.com
Chahboun, I. (n.d.). Retrieved from www.pinterest.com
Chaplin, C. (n.d.). Retrieved from www.quotes-central.com
Churchill, W. (n.d.). Retrieved from likesuccess.com
Coelho, P. (n.d.). Retrieved from www.pinterest.com
Coelho, P. (2013, 10 25). http://paulocoelhoblog.com/2013/10/25/the-child-within-us/. Retrieved from Paulo Coelho Writer Official Site: http://paulocoelhoblog.com/
Cooley, M. (n.d.). Retrieved from designedbykrystleblog.com
Deborah Fox. (n.d.). Retrieved from www.quotehd.com
DeWalt J. (n.d.). Retrieved from www.picturequotes.com
Einstein, A. (n.d.). Retrieved from www.quotesvalley.com
Einstein, A. (n.d.). Retrieved from www.azquotes.com
Elmore, K. (n.d.). Retrieved from http://www.goodreads.com/quotes/
Ferriss, T. (n.d.). Retrieved from blog.jwashburn.com
Foer, J. S. (n.d.). Retrieved from quotesgram.com
Foer, J. S. (n.d.). Retrieved from topfamousquotes.com
Ford, H. (n.d.). Retrieved from www.slideshare.net
Graham, M. (n.d.). Retrieved from www.slideshare.net
Guillemets, T. (n.d.). Retrieved from www.pinterest.com
Hoebel, B. (n.d.). Retrieved from www.pinterest.com
Huxley, A. (n.d.). Retrieved from quotefancy.com
Ionesco, E. (n.d.). Retrieved from izquotes.com
Jr., M. L. (n.d.). Retrieved from www.yoddler.com
Keillor, G. (n.d.). Retrieved from www.pinterest.com
Lange, C. L. (n.d.). Retrieved from izquotes.com
Lee, B. (n.d.). Retrieved from plus.google.com
Levenson, S. (n.d.). Retrieved from imgfave.com
Lindqvist, J. A. (n.d.). Retrieved from quotesjunk.com
Lobowitz, F. (n.d.). Retrieved from izquotes.com
Mandela, N. (n.d.). Retrieved from http://londonlifejournal.blogspot.in/
Marino, D. (n.d.). Retrieved from www.pinterest.com

Martin, G. R. (n.d.). Retrieved from www.pinterest.com
McKain, N. (n.d.). Retrieved from www.jarofquotes.com
Morpurgo, M. (n.d.). Retrieved fromwww.azquotes.com
Nesselroad, L. (n.d.). Retrieved from www.pinterest.com
Niven, S. M. (n.d.). Retrieved from www.quotehd.com
Oppenhemier, R. (n.d.). Retrieved from izquotes.com
Ortberg, J. (n.d.). Retrieved from www.goodreads.com
Picasso, P. (n.d.). Retrieved from www.picturequotes.com
Poindexter, L. (n.d.). Retrieved from boardofwisdom.com
Pollan, M. (n.d.). Retrieved from www.pinterest.com
Proverb. (n.d.). Retrieved from quotesgram.com
Proverb, C. (n.d.). Retrieved from www.slideshare.net
Proverb, J. (n.d.). Retrieved from www.pinterest.com
Proverb, T. (n.d.). Retrieved from quotesgram.com
Pulitzer, L. (n.d.). Retrieved from www.kateathome.com
Rivkin, S. (n.d.). Retrieved from www.pinterest.com
Rohn, J. (n.d.). Retrieved from quotefancy.com
Rumi. (n.d.). Retrieved from andthenwesaved.com
Samuel Johnson. (n.d.). Retrieved from izquotes.com
Seuss, D. (n.d.). Retrieved from www.pinterest.com
Shaw, G. B. (n.d.). Retrieved from twitter.com
Sinatra, F. (n.d.). Retrieved from www.quotehd.com.
Sliter, M. (n.d.). Retrieved from www.pinterest.com
Swindoll, C. R. (n.d.). Retrieved from quotes.lifehack.org
Terrany, J. (n.d.). Retrieved from www.pinterest.com
Thoreau, H. D. (n.d.). Retrieved from quotesgram.com
Tjoe, C. (n.d.). Retrieved from boardofwisdom.com
Wells, O. (n.d.). Retrieved from thearisgold.com
Wigmore, A. (n.d.). Retrieved from www.pinterest.com
Winfrey, O. (n.d.). Retrieved from free-quotes.xyz

================